Journal

OF A

Madman

Journal

OF A

Madman

Ryan Szeto

iUniverse, Inc.
Bloomington

Journal of a Madman

iUniverse books may be ordered through booksellers or by contacting:

iUniverse
1663 Liberty Drive
Bloomington, IN 47403
www.iuniverse.com
1-800-Authors (1-800-288-4677)

ISBN: 978-1-4759-2755-9 (sc)
ISBN: 978-1-4759-2756-6 (ebk)

Printed in the United States of America

iUniverse rev. date: 05/21/2012

Contents

Preface

First and foremost, thank you for purchasing this book and taking interest in who I am and what I went through in the last few years to conjure up these pages.

It took a lot of strife and heartache to type all these words that you are about to read and thusly, I hope you can find where these lines fit in your life. I just hope that I wasn't the only one that went through all of that pain for nothing. Just take into consideration that each poem that I wrote was a chapter in my life and think of each of them as another chapter in a book. I realize after typing all of this down, each poem sounded like a modern version of Edgar Allen Poe. Another person mentioned to me that the poems as a whole read very much like Jack Kerouac's book "On the road". This whole book wasn't considered to be a collection of poems or even a journal. It just so happens to be a journal my life in the past few years and just happens to be written as poems. Each poem that a wrote came from the heart and the moment. Each time I put words down, it was another drop of blood and another tear that fell onto these pages. People always told me that everyone hurts and I just decided to put it down in word form. All I want you to know is that I'm human just like you and society just happen to keep picking at me till I broke down. Just enough to write how I felt. I guess you can say that this was the pillow that I cried into every night. The main purpose I wrote all this down was to release some anger and frustration. Thinking back on all of it, I just want people to understand that all you say and do can hurt others. I just hope that these writings brings some peace to you and the people around you.

Burden

Being blind all these years hurts
Love blinds me to who I am
I love to much
It hurts to much
It's a noose that hangs me
Everyone tells me my heart will be someone's
Someday
I don't think it'll happen
Every time I love someone
I care for someone
It falls apart
It doesn't matter if I'm in a relationship
It burdens me so much
Drives me insane
Why was I cursed with such a great heart
Why couldn't I just be some heartless bastard
Just fucking someone and moving on
I loathe myself
I can't ask someone to kill me
Nor can I ask myself to take my life
I just want someone to share my love
So I don't have to be in so much pain
The pain I cause myself

Bloody Pages

What happens to me when I start writing
I spill my heart and soul
Just everything I have to offer
On these pages
I bleed so much on these pages
I don't know who I am anymore
Every step I take in life
Seeing that nothing is perfect anymore
Maybe you can see your own feelings
Amongst these pages
Every word that I write
Every tear soaked page
Written in blood
I wait for someone to come along
To read all these words that consume me
My fears
My losses
I'm bound to a broken heart
That bleeds for you
To be there
I forget the pain
When I write on these pages

It's a burden that I carry
The thoughts of you
Wanders through my heart
Only reason I write because I love
Until I stop wandering
Till I come home
Into your arms
Until then
I keep writing
Keep bleeding on these pages
My heart aches
Everyday that I'm away from you
You are my home
My hope
The complete joy in my life
You would never understand
How much I want you in my life
I will always feel incomplete without you
It forces me to bleed more
Life seems to turn a page
Turns a blind eye to this bloody page

Cold Nights

Moving on
Growing cold
No one calls
They never do
No one ever does
I always end up calling someone

There are cold nights
Without you
With you here
I wouldn't need to stand here
Alone
In the dark

The only thing I need
Is your love
To guide my heart
To warm my heart
Every little word
That you say
That you don't say
Makes my nights so much warmer

For some reason
Your love shows me the way
With that
My love can shine
Show everybody else
How to love
Show the world
It's what we need

Useless

I don't want to get old
Where I become useless
When I can't do anything
For anyone
Even for myself
Will you still call me
When you need help
I feel so useless when you don't
What is a friend suppose to do
When you don't even call on them
I'll always be that soldier standing guard
When you need me
But I can't believe you don't even call on me
I feel so useless
I'm getting older
Useless
When time takes me
And I haven't fulfilled my duty
I stand here
Heartbroken
When you don't call

It kills me when I can't do anything for you
The only reason I live
Is for you
No one else
I'll carry you under my wing
I'll always be right here
Always on guard
Always on call
It always seems useless
To stand here
When no one calls
The only use I have is to be here
Waiting
Giving
Not getting anything in return
Give up all that matters
Besides being there
Everything else is useless to me
Even myself

Lonely home

It feels so good to be home
Somewhere familiar
Somewhere safe
But something is still missing
It's that empty feeling inside
That I originally ran from
It still lingers around
My shadow that I can't shake
I still felt like I had a purpose when I moved
To find myself

I helped others find something
I forget sometimes why I'm lonely
It's because of my love for you
I love you too much
I could never shake the feeling that I left you
Just wish I could have that love
Constantly by my side
The true home is in my heart
Alone

In the dark still crying in the corner
Wish I could be the one in your life to love you forever
Just wish we could accept things
The things that we do
And who we are
For the love that we give

Living Hell

Why do I live in my own hell
Why do I loathe myself so much
When I hate all this so much
It scares me so
I can't sleep when I know
That I'm so alone
I don't feel enough to cry
Not enough to cry for you
I'm so numb
Numb by my own loneliness
I hate the memories of you that linger
I want you by me but I don't know
If I can have you close by
I despise myself that I don't know if I hate you
Or love you
Oh god someone help me
Hold me
All I see around me is hell's fire
Please, someone come for me and lend me a hand
I need someone
That soft touch

Angel's heaven

I'm looking out to the night sky
Knowing my love is out there
I got no gold
Besides her love

Her touch
Soft skin
But nothing's better
Then her love
It completes me
Knowing that I can look at those stars
Having a love of an angel
I wonder sometimes
Where this angel came from

Knowing that I don't deserve this
But it feels so good
I'm so grateful to have her
Finally having her in my arms

This must be an angel's heaven
I must be up there
In their heaven
Loving no matter what
Protect me from all other harms

Faceless hero

There are heroes out there
You don't see them
You can never see their face
But we'll always be there
With love
We guard this country of ours

Beyond those city lights
We sit and wait
To protect
To serve
For those brothers, sisters
We shelter the ones we love

I feel stronger now
Protecting you
I followed through
You're under my wing
It fulfills my duty
I can die happy
Loving you
Protecting you

Although most people would never see my face
Pray that you will never need me
You will probably never see me
Walking next to you
But I'm right here
With love

I stand guard
With many others
To protect what we love
Just know that we're there
I love you
I don't expect much
Except that joy
Of thanks on your face
I will love you no matter what

Settled Cowboy

Been traveling alone for too long
Been wandering
Tired of traveling
Tired of being alone

I made one stop
Saw you
Didn't think of anything
At first
Then you said hello
Saw pain in my eyes
Thought I needed a friend
You were right

My life on the road was like water
An ocean that hasn't been settled
But you settled it
Settled my heart
Calmed this untamed pain
I thank you
For being there
Always

Now
I want to be there for you
You mean everything
This love has settled me
This wave has hit the shore
You changed me
Wanting to just be by you
Slowing down and enjoying
The sun is setting on this old cowboy
Couldn't be better

Along Came a Spider

What happens if you never met me
Would your life be the same
Would you know that I existed
Would you believe that real heroes existed

Then I came along
Did you ever think
Guys like me existed

People say that you'd marry someone great
Best thing ever
I guess I can match it

Sometimes I'm looked over
People not knowing who I am
Not taking a second glance
Everyone always takes a look
When a spider comes along
Across your path

When that happens
You might realize how great
That one spider could be
You also might fear it
It's all up to you

You can either kill me
Miss out on something great
Like I was some insignificant little spider
You might realize how great this little spider can me
A great hero
Because this little spider
Has one gigantic heart
You might not want to miss it

Little Boy

Why is it that I call attention to myself
I cry out like a little boy
Then run away
There are times when people call attention
To all my faults
When one person starts it
Everyone picks on me

I just don't get why one person
Can start a ripple effect and shove me into a corner
All I ask sometimes is just an opinion
It's an idiotic question
But people can be cruel
Picking at the little things
Not even answering the question

Makes me cry at night
It rains in my head
Especially when I just ask a simple question
It's just stupid how people can rip me apart
Make me bleed
For something as stupid as a simple thought

Fuck people
For those who don't care
Just rip me to shreds

Not caring
Unrelenting pain
Knowing how cruel the world is
For all I've done for others
What I always get in return
Shit thrown in my face

All I do is be
I always get knocked down
Dirt in my face
Humiliated like I always do
Making me feel like a little boy
Crying
Feels like grade school again
People pointing
Laughing
Seeing how much of a dunce I am
Can't live like this

Where's my hero to save me
I need that hero to hold me
Save me
Stop me from crying
I don't deserve this

Courage

What does it take to be a hero
To love, never ending
To care about anyone
No matter what

This love has to be great
Has to be over the limit of what is expected
You have to be willing to give your life
For love
People have to be more important
You're not as important as others
Give more than take
Graciousness is the most important part of being a hero
The courage to do so counts

But being this part is not easy
The questions keep coming
What do I get
Nothing
Just a thanks
Know that you did your job
Also dealing with the pain of doing the right thing
Just knowing that you could've saved that one poor soul
Sometimes you just want to know if you're doing the right thing
Wonder if there's any more you can do for others

Everyone needs a hero
Someone they could look for
Just someone to hope that they can see again
It takes bravery
Courage
A lot of love to know what it takes
Love cures and saves us all but the hero

When a hero questions himself
People always wonder where he's gone to
I just want someone to look up to
Everyone loves a hero

There's a hero in all of us
I just want to tell you
Just to hold on a little longer
I'll always be there
I think I can die with pride
Knowing I did something right
People need a hero and I need you
I'm proud of what I done for you

Run

I've been running from myself for way to long
I didn't know who I was
I found out who I am
I found out that there is much more
A whole lot of people who need me
I ran to some great friends but it's time for me
Just to run
I don't want to run away
It just feels so good to have some great friends
Just know that I'll be there in your heart
A hero will always be there for you
I know you would spend countless hours
Staring at that moonlit sky just waiting for a glimpse of your hero
Your great friend
Although I'm not physically there
I'll try my best to come to you if you ever
I mean ever need me
I'm devoted to taking care of you
I found a harmony in my life

My life is both a major and minor key
All my life, it was a minor key
I found that major key
That is you
My close friends
I love you
You should all know that

Give

I give so much away
I have nothing left for myself
I sacrifice all of my being
Is there anything left for me
It takes the breathe out of me
It just seems I can't live for myself
How can I save others
When I can't even save myself
It just feels so cold
Sometimes
I just don't know
Lost in my own thoughts
Pain
Finds me
Deals a fatal blow to my heart
I know I'm loved
It feels like it's not enough
I suppose I'm not excepting it
I should open my heart to love
I've given so much love
I don't know how to except it
I don't know why
I just feel so empty for some reason
Just show me how my life ends
Show me how happy I am
I want to feel joy again

That pure joy that surrounds me
When will it just be alright
Why do I always dance with myself
I hate this bugging thought
That always follows me
When I hit that road
It always follows
That shadow that clings to my shoes
I can't run from my own pains
Have no fucking clue why I can't shake myself
Will someone just fucking stab an axe in my back
To make the god damn pain go away
It's the only way I can ease my pain
The only cure is having my love
My love for you
Will break my heart in two
If you should fall
It would crumble so easily
Like a flower
Someone just hold me
Save me
I don't deserve this pain
This guilt of what I've done
The pain of living when I should've died

The Memories

The presence of you remains in my heart
Every part of your kindness lingers
Why do I still think of you
It doesn't matter anymore
It's your distant voice that stays
Just don't listen to that distant thunder
It's a freight train to my heart
It just doesn't feel right like this
It feels like hope has left me when great friends leave me
My heart bleeds knowing I couldn't help you
That I couldn't be by your side forever
To protect you from harm
I guess I was just a hero for a day
What is a hero to do when a hero can't save one person
I wish I could have done better
I lost a soul
I can still hear that cry for help
Helping so many doesn't cut it anymore
I couldn't save just one more
I don't consider myself a savior
I'm no preacher
Nothing more
I do my best to be a friend
A kind person who's willing to protect
I'd give anything for you
But I just feel like I'm not wanted

I know some say no
There are some that didn't want my help
All I really had was good intentions
All that's left of my heart is left out there
On that road
I just feel like an outlaw again
Torn to pieces
I waited my whole life
For someone that would save me
I just feel like I'm wasting my time
I just feel better dying behind the wheel
Just looking for someone
Myself
Would you look for me
Am I worth looking for
Called out for
I don't want that time to be ticking away
I just want to smash that clock because I fear
I fear my own death before I was meant for nothing good
Not anymore

Battling the odds with myself

What good am I
What am I supposed to do
I'm patient but I don't have much time left
It's my world
I keep myself busy to the fact that I can't sit still
Can someone slow me down
I want to just enjoy life
There's a couple of people out there that can do that
Time seems to just slow down when I'm with you
Just know that this slow sanity comes to a screeching stop
Only when you're here with me
When I hear your sweet voice
To hold you
To know that I did something great for you
I love you for that
For making me laugh
To make me realize that there's nothing left
Left in this world besides just you and me
I'm just waiting for time to stop completely so I can be with you
For eternity
I love you

Forget

I know I forget sometimes
There's no one in town
You let me in
I forgot why
You took care of me
I forgot to thank you for that
You were so kind to me
I never appreciated it
What would you think of me now
You were such a great friend
It's too late now
May angels lead you in
I was never really there for you
It pains me to have done so
I want to forget the pain
If you were with me
I would sing for you one last time
For a heart so big
God won't let it live
I feel that it's not enough
It's never enough for the pain I live with everyday
It pains me that I was never there for you
I try to be better
I try to be better for the next person
I wish I did more for you
It seems that it's never enough

It wasn't enough
Please forgive me for what I've done
I never got an answer
Since you're gone
For some reason you would answer
To tell me that it's ok
It wasn't my fault
I know that you'd be proud of me
I was always proud of you
I'm happy and hope you're somewhere better
I'm so sorry that I couldn't be there for you
Just know
I'm happy to have had you as my best friend
With the time we had together

Do you really want to know

Do you want me to show you my life
Do you want me to show you my hopes
My dreams
My desire
Just let me tell you the things that are real to me
Let me share my dreams
Hopes and need to reach the sky
It's what I've been dreaming about for ages
I need to reach it because it's the ultimate goal
To die happy and successful
It's my way to break these chains in my life
To break all these curses I deal with
My salvation is up there
Will you join me for the journey
Are you worthy to be part of my clan
One of the many hordes of people who reach for that sky
Do you want me to take you
My soul is being reincarnated
I feel free again
But hope is still too far away
I always need you to give me a hand to throw me back up
into the sky
My clan will always be the ones I love the most
I just don't want to disappoint any of you

Tell me that
I just want to know that I'm never a disappointment
It breaks my heart and will always make me fall once again
I just need someone to save me
To save me from this hell I know as myself
You're love always shines through and reigns through to my heart
I'll always keep you close and love you for it

Heart of a hero

Someone falls down
A heart falls
Someone looses hope

I will be there to pick up the pieces
To hold you
To kiss you
Everyone has a hero
I'll be that hero for you

I hope my heart covers your pain
It feels like I'm not doing enough
Is there anything I can do to make you feel great
Make you feel like you're in heaven
I'll give you my whole being
I just want some love in return

Who's going to save me
Who's going to give me some love
I'm always searching for someone
Some kind of love

Do I just walk off after I saved someone
Just be a hero for a day
Do I just love then leave
No, that's not me
I love with all my heart
I just want you to accept it

All I ask is some love in return

Broken Hero

Do I love too much
All I want to know is that you're safe
I don't want to say I'm a savior
I just love too much
I hit this dark highway to often
I just try to help and show you my love
I always end up screwing things up
I've been hurt by worse
The things you do
Doesn't affect me
I'm numb from the pain when you don't accept my love
I'm always trying my best to be a hero
But there's only so much I can do
When will someone save me
Save me from my own pains
There are people who love me
But is that love true
I don't know if I can let my guard down just yet
My trust has been broken
Just know I love you with all my being
Just show me a little love

Is it me?

I'm trying to make this life make sense
I miss the way that love feels
I'm so far away from it all
That light is fading
I forget how it feels
I forget that happiness covers all pain
But the feelings gone
There's nothing to lift me up
How am I to find the way
When I can't even help myself
I lose sight of my angel
I'm so lost that I can't even tell what I've done
Please, shine some of your love down to me
That bright love of yours makes my spirit high
I can breathe again knowing that I have you by my side
lifting me up
By no means is my love for you gone
My love for you will always be here
All I seek is some good love in return

Since I fell

Ever since I fell in love
I never knew that I change every time that I do
My heart drops every time I don't hear from you
I feel like I'm the best of fools
When I force myself into love
It breaks my soul to know
That I'm too damned arrogant
I'm just a fool to know that love can be a waste
I still know what I feel for you is true
My love will always stay true for you
Just know that I care for you no matter what
It's the only thing that keeps me alive
If I love you
It gives me a purpose
My love for you
Helps you
It makes you always feel better
That is the purpose in my life
As long as you know that
It keeps me sane
It keeps me alive
All I ask sometimes is a little love in return
I can fall without it

Once my heart falls
That will make me tumble and loose my purpose
Just tell me that I'm needed
So I can thank the ones I love
I love you so much that you won't believe

True friend

You're that one true friend that stuck by me
I trust you with everything
I love everything about you
I love you like a sister

I always want to be there for you
You take so much love out of me
I don't know if there's much left of me
I'm willing to do anything for you

I'll always be here to support you in every little way
Every part of me I give you
You mean everything to me
Everyday to every breath I take
My heart knows no bounds

Just promise
Promise that you could be better
Better then you say you are
I always want the best for you
You are the best thing that came into my life
Stay safe

I promise

I promised that I will see you again
I promised that I'd be your friend till the end
I told you that I'd be there through the bitter end
Although it breaks my heart that you don't remember me
I'll keep my promise
I'd promise that I am willing to die for you
I promise that you have my heart

I will always welcome you with open arms
I will always look up at those stars and think of you
You're the best thing that happened to me
I hope that I am the same for you

Look up at those stars
Do I come up at least once
Do you wonder what I'm up to
Do you wish I was by your side
It might be more than just a thought

What does your heart say
I always welcome love
If it's not that kind of love
I don't mind
As long as it's love that you find
That your trust is involved

Although I'm not perfect
We aren't exactly the best at being human
I'll be here right here waiting for you to trust me
Just don't be condescending with your troubles
I'll always find the words
I've always made the commitment to you

With arms wide open
I'll always be here to care for you
I'll be that angel that watches over you

Who's going to love me
There are days I wish someone will save me
Please love me
I can always care for you
Love is needed
Karma is bound to follow me back

I will always be here to give you a kiss good night
Just be safe

The fallen heart

To the one I could have loved
I was beginning to trust you
I was willing to give you all my secrets
Just as I was about to give you my heart
You left me
I still don't understand entirely why
I called out to you but you never answered
I just figured it was something I said
Are you scared of me
Do you hate me
I still don't know
I just wanted to know the reason
I was willing and ready to love you
With all my heart
Just come back to me please

To whom it may concern

My love
I will always miss the way you feel
My love
I'm afraid I don't know you anymore
My mind says one thing
It doesn't know where you went
My heart is left torn and tattered
I know I will never be the same without you
I could move on but what is the point
No one out there realizes that I'm here anymore
Who comes here to hold me
Who comes to save me
Who comes to pick up the pieces of my heart
No one
I'm not the victim when I know I did the harm
I know I made the mistake
Everything I do hurts the ones I love
I can't stop bleeding
The wounds won't close
Although I can still feel you're touch
I don't think I'll ever be ready to go back
Don't think I'll stay around this town much longer
There's nothing for me here now
That dark highway always waits for me

Just cause no one can give me grief but myself
It's the road I choose and I can't change
It will be a never ending remembrance when you're sweetness
will never leave
Those hearts I have will always be with me
There's only one reason why I wear my hearts on my sleeve
It's a very dangerous thing to do so
I will always love before thinking
I have no control over it
Is there someone to return my love without remorse
Please someone be you
Those friends that can trust love one last time
I don't know if I want to give love one more try
I'll always hope

You're not here

I don't want to lose that feeling
Please don't leave me again
I lost to many people along this road
I always meet people along the way
Every time I do, I wonder how long they will stay
Are they here to just enjoy the ride
Are they here for the long haul
I just want to find some company
I might have just found someone
I almost feel whole when you're around
I still have my doubts
Hope is clouding my doubts
I have faith that this bond might hold
Only reason I feel this way is that it feels right when you're around
When you're gone, it makes me want you closer to me
Please don't leave me
To the friends I hold dear
I love all of you

Tired

I'm so tired
Tired of living
Breathing
Hurting
I believe I'm cursed
To live with a heart so big
Tired of living with people
Tired of them telling me
That I'm not good enough
Not strong enough
I'm tired of myself
Tired of myself holding me down
What can I do
When no one wants to lend me a hand
I gave so much
It doesn't help me when they give me a hand
Then let me go

When I can trust
They let me go
I can't trust anyone
So tired
Tired of trusting others
I shouldn't have trusted
It was better not to trust
Trusting is for the weak
No one needs friends
When the only friends of mine
Are the ones in my head
The ones I know
So tired
I should just take what I can get
Give nothing back

Me

I'm no hero
I'm nothing more than just a little boy
I enjoy life
I laugh at the little things
But I crave attention
I can't stand being alone
But when I get angry
I need to be alone
I'm so conflicted with what's right
With who I am
I hate capitalism
But I live with it
I love life
But I loathe it
I'm no hero
I just have a big heart
I'm just here to do a job
I'm here to care about whomever crosses my path
That's the only thing I'm good at
That's the only thing I know
People don't understand me
Say that I'm crazy
Weird
But the sad thing is
I don't even understand myself
I spend days on end

Trying to figure out who I am
I know where I belong in life
My true goal in life
Admiration
It's the only thing I'm sure of
Acceptance
It's what feeds my need
The adoring love of people
That would bring me peace
Nothing else matters
It's the only thing that can bring a smile
On this wrinkled face of mine
Only wrinkled by madness
The sadness that shrouds my existence
I only ask for people to just put up with me
Don't bother me if you don't want my burden
It's a hard journey
But I need you
Nothing else can be ever be better

Journey for Heart

My sorrows will never end
I lose so many
This journey is so perilous
It hurts that I don't have you
I'm glad for the few that stayed
I always think about you
Although I lost you
I can't stop thinking about you
I've lost you for all time
I just think of the good times
Pray that you're in a better place
I've always pushed you up before myself
But I just want to be with you
When can someone pick me up
I pray that our hearts can tangle
I can't do it with you
I can't finish it without you
I need you here by me
To finish this journey
To get to a goal
To reach that light
You're undying love
I need so much
Because it's hard to reach the stars
You're the only one that makes me remember to bring my chin up

To remind me what I'm shooting for
To look up and reach for those stars
I need you by my side
I can't help thinking that we went separate ways
That we grew apart
Like our past never happened
I just know in my heart that we are meant to cross again
Continue the journey that our hearts have started
I just wish our hearts will blend again
Now I step forward to realize this wish
Is it true that it has started
Has it ended because of fear
Don't be afraid
My heart will lift you into the light
Just take my hand
I just want to be with you now
Everyone is always meant to be as one together

Empty Heart

I need love
I want love
My heart is so empty
I just need something to fill it back up
It's the feeling that still remains
I don't need your charity
It's not why I'm here
I just need those three words
It's a miracle that you came here
Just a look into your eyes
Fills my heart
The way you say those words
Fills me with such joy
I'm so addicted to your love
The day you don't say it
The day ends

I fall back into darkness
I just want your love
But for some reason I don't think it's enough sometimes
I need an ocean's worth
It's still not enough to fill my heart
There's still holes in my heart
I need you to patch it up
Be there
Dry up my tears
It fills me with desire
I need a miracle
I need you
To refill this empty heart

Astray

I always felt alone
Astray from the pack
Astray from logic
Gone from sanity
I wandered away from that light
It's a never ending movie
The house lights never come up
Life seems so fleeting
Astray from who I really am
Doubt has led me astray
To my brain
I feel so estranged from it all
Being that my heart will always hurt
I can't forgive you
When I can't forgive myself
I need to move away from all my guilt
Move away from my home
Move away from my pain
Go astray from my true pains
I want to run away from myself again
I need to find myself
How is this suppose to work
Help me figure myself out

Never Loose

Another day comes to an end
Another late night
Just you think things will end
It starts all over again
The sun comes out
It starts all over again
I thought I could lose it all the night before
It just starts again
But I never give up
Keep plugging away
Be a wolf in sheep's clothing
Plow through the field of sheep
Be somebody
On my own
Just never let up
I'm determined
To find what I'm looking for
Never let down
I'm just out there on my own
To be someone
Never to be someone else
I've got my own dreams to accomplish
To know I've done something for myself
To prove to myself that I could be somebody
Not to prove anyone else anything
Just to know I'm something

In you I trust

I was always here waiting
Thinking that you would trust
Trust me with your sorrows
Trust me with things that bother you
Do years pass you by
Do we finally come face to face
With a blank stare on our faces
With a look of distrust
Do you not trust me
Is it that I'm asking you to listen
Is it too much to ask
I was always here listening
But when I ask you to listen
Just once
Was it just too much for you
I told you when we met
I carry the burden of the world
I always carry on without you

But you will never understand
Never see that I give my all
It comes with the territory
But it's never enough
You just want me to shut up
There are days when I kick myself
Hearing what people say
That I'm not good enough

I shut them out and just keep moving
Because its never enough until I reach the top
I will never be done until I reach the end
Find that heart of gold
I want to always live
To give and reach it
Smile on me deathbed knowing that I've done everything
I don't need you anymore
Holding me down

Mad Liar

Don't know why I do the things I do
I lie to others to get recognition
Always looking for attention
Because I'm crying inside
Crying out for attention
It's an unnamed feeling
No matter where I go
I've been there before
But I always know that feeling
It's always comes alive
Because it always eats at me
With these maddening lies
It eats me inside
In all ways, shapes and forms
I just want some attention

I look happy at times
But when you look into my eyes
Shows my pain
Wanting to be in someone's arms
Being with someone
I want to run out of my body
I loathe this feeling
I want to get out of this body
I want to forget
Remembering brings so much pain
Fucking hate this feeling
With pain, anger and sadness
It all takes me away into a dark place
I just don't want to be here anymore

Life Changes

Every day changes
Plans fail
Life comes and goes
Could I forgive myself
Move on
Change what I've said
What I've done
I wouldn't change anything
Except forgive myself
I wouldn't turn the clock back
Change what I've said
Most of the things I've said
I meant
It's up to you to accept it
The one thing in life I could change
Is myself
Just to let go and forgive the one person in my life

Myself
It's the biggest thing I could do
No one can change it but me
I don't deserve this punishment
Cursed with a heart so big
That cares
Bleeds
Tired of having so much humility
It's the aspect of the human condition
People tell me I should move on
Let it all go
It's what makes me remember
So I won't forget which road to take
When I come to those crossroads
When things get troubled
That's where I can make the change
It's the choices we make

Shifts

When the lights go out
The sun comes out
There has been cold nights
The sun shifts upwards
I just want to be there
Walking the streets of my city
I realize I'm home
Where I belong
On the cold dark night
It feels right being here
I know nothing else
It fills the void
There's still something missing
That emptiness inside
Those feelings of regret
Loneliness
Happiness
I know I'm meant for something

I just don't know what
There's always something
Everyone comes to me
Shifting me back to do something
Just tired of listening to others
Just let me be
Let me collect my thoughts
Let me be myself
Just feels like a shifting tide
It comes to me in one swoop
Then takes awhile to leave me
When I think it's all over
It starts over again
I can't run from it
It seems like it never ends
All I ask is to be left alone
Just let me be

Devil's Doorstep

Staring at the devil
Square in the eyes
Thinking about the world at hand
Nothing makes sense
Taking responsibility for everything
Like Atlas with the world on his shoulders
Asking so many questions
That have no answers
Just don't understand what's going on
Always taking two steps forward
Then four steps back
Can't move forward
Set back by others in need
Feels like all of the world's burden

The devil's pain pulls me back
How can the world's pain
Come at me all at once
My room
My world
Just keeps spinning
Makes me dizzy
Just need someone to hold me still
I don't know if I can succeed
Caught up in so much misery
Can't stand it anymore
Can't stand on my own two feet anymore
The devil's pain burns a hole

Ending Beginning,
Beginning End

Another year comes and goes
I'm going the wrong way
Down a one way track
Always fighting upstream
One against the world
Will there ever be a beginning
My candle still burns
In this ever darkening world
The wax burns to nothing
It still burns
Never fading
There's not much left
Still burning
I'll still fight myself
Still trek upstream
I'll still fight for what I believe
Until someone comes along
So that my fire can light their way
Till the end
To show you the beginning
To light the end
It will always burn
For the ones I love

The Beaten

Battling constantly
Doing for others
Nothing accomplished
Never thought of myself
I always thought of others
Looks like misery
No one will understand
Understand what I put myself though
To do things for others
A devotion and love
Beaten down
By burden
Scarred by love
Makes me weirder
With all this that kills me
It's a fight till the end
There are always times
Everyday
That I can't forgive myself
For loving to much
I soak in my own misery
Everyday
Everyone tells me to stop killing myself
Stop beating myself over the head
I can't help it
I can't stop

Being who I am
Tell someone to stop caring
To stop loving
I'm just bleeding to death
No one realizes it
I kill myself
Sacrifice myself
To make someone else's life better
Nothing else really matters

Plays Life, Plays You

Trying to get a hold on life
Trying to make sense of things
Thought I had a hold on what was real
What I knew fell apart
Nothing I do makes sense
You think you understand life
Life understands you more
It figures out that you don't matter
You're just a speck of dust
In the greater void
Of nothingness
Just figured that I try to be happy
Just for this moment in time
Nothing else matters
Our lives are just to short
Even if you leave a mark on this world
Life turns a blind eye and doesn't care
You're just nothing
Just live and be happy

Wasted days

Could I have those wasted days back
Should I use them to get my life back
To get back on track
Everything so crazy
Just feels like I'm wasting time
Doesn't feel like I'm getting anywhere in life
Just floating by
I just keep searching
The search for meaning
Making some kind of sense of it all
I just need to make sense of it all
Do I really have the strength
To make sense of things
Everything just feels so dirty
Just want to shed off all this anger
All of this unwanted shame
The things that I hate
My temple is clean inside
But punch drunk dirty on the outside
Just to much pent up aggression
Need some release
Need to look out the dirty window
To see myself and how clean it is

Burning Forgiveness

It's so hard to leave this regret
Old memories flood back
It always feels like I'm carrying the world
I dedicated my life to all
Except myself
I battle constantly
Always helping others
Never for myself
I never let anyone carry my burdens
Never undoing those chains
Burn me till I have nothing left
It just pains me that all I do
Is never good enough
It's never what you wanted
When all I did was always for you
How can I forgive myself
When all I do for you
Was never good enough
I give everything to everyone
But it's never good enough
Just forgive me for being human

How it is

It never surprises me
The things that you've done to me
Pains me
Gave an enormous effort to you
I did everything for you
What did you do for me
It wasn't me
No matter how hard I tried
You just threw it back in my face
You said you loved me
You really didn't know how you hurt me
Everyday you said that you hated drama
You hated liars
You couldn't handle the truth I fed you
You said I was needy
I just wanted you

To devote a little time
For all I gave you
I just saw something in your eyes
You never wanted anything to do with me
All this didn't break me
It pissed me off
I wasted time and effort on you
I cared about you but you lied to me
If you didn't want any part of me
You should have told me
You're the biggest hypocrite I know
Hope you find out the hard way in life
You're empty inside
Just don't come crying to me when you find out

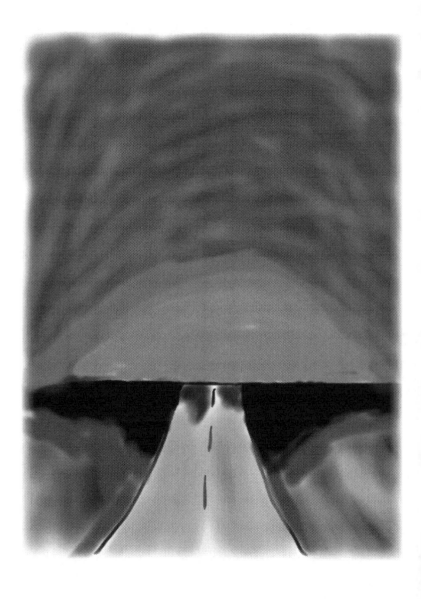